# United States Presidents

## John Tyler

Anne Welsbacher
ABDO Publishing Company

192
TYLER

**visit us at**
**www.abdopub.com**

Published by ABDO Publishing Company 4940 Viking Drive, Edina, Minnesota 55435.


Printed in the United States.

Photo credits: Archive Photos, UPI/Corbis-Bettmann

Contributing editors: Robert Italia, Tamara L. Britton, K.M. Brielmaier, Kate A. Furlong

**Library of Congress Cataloging-in-Publication Data**

Welsbacher, Anne, 1955-
John Tyler / Anne Welsbacher.
p. cm. -- (United States presidents)
Includes index.
Summary: A biography of the Virginian who became tenth president of the United States upon the death of William Henry Harrison.
ISBN 1-57765-239-8
1. Tyler, John, 1790-1862--Juvenile literature. 2. Presidents--United States--Biography--Juvenile literature. [1. Tyler, John, 1790-1862. 2. Presidents.] I. Title. II. Series: United States presidents (Edina, Minn.)
E397.W45 1999
973.5'8'092--dc21
[B] 98-20924
CIP
AC

# Contents

# John Tyler

John Tyler was born in Virginia in 1790. At the age of 19, he became a lawyer. Later, he became a member of the U.S. **House of Representatives**, governor of Virginia, and a U.S. Senator.

In 1840, William Henry Harrison was elected president. Tyler was elected vice president. But President Harrison died just one month after taking office. A president had never died in office before.

**Congress** was not sure whether the vice president became president, or if they needed to elect a new one. Tyler said he should be president according to the Constitution. Because of his decision, when the president dies, the vice president becomes president.

Many lawmakers did not accept that Tyler was truly the president. Tyler had a lot of trouble with **Congress** and his **cabinet**. He retired after one term as president. He died in 1862.

John Tyler

# *John Tyler* (1790-1862)
## Tenth President

| | |
|---|---|
| BORN: | March 29, 1790 |
| PLACE OF BIRTH: | Charles City County, Virginia |
| ANCESTRY: | English |
| FATHER: | John Tyler (1747-1813) |
| MOTHER: | Mary Marot Armistead Tyler (1761-1797) |
| WIVES: | First wife: Letitia Christian (1790-1842)<br>Second wife: Julia Gardiner (1820-1889) |
| CHILDREN: | First wife: 3 boys, 5 girls<br>Second wife: 5 boys, 2 girls |
| EDUCATION: | Local Virginia schools, College of William and Mary |
| RELIGION: | Episcopalian |
| OCCUPATION: | Lawyer |
| MILITARY SERVICE: | Captain of volunteer company in Richmond, Virginia |
| POLITICAL PARTY: | Democrat, later a Whig |

| | |
|---|---|
| OFFICES HELD: | Member of Virginia Legislature, member of U.S. House of Representatives, governor of Virginia, U.S. senator, vice president |
| AGE AT INAUGURATION: | 51 |
| YEARS SERVED: | 1841-1845 |
| VICE PRESIDENT: | None |
| DIED: | January 18, 1862, Richmond, Virginia, age 71 |
| CAUSE OF DEATH: | Illness due to bronchitis |

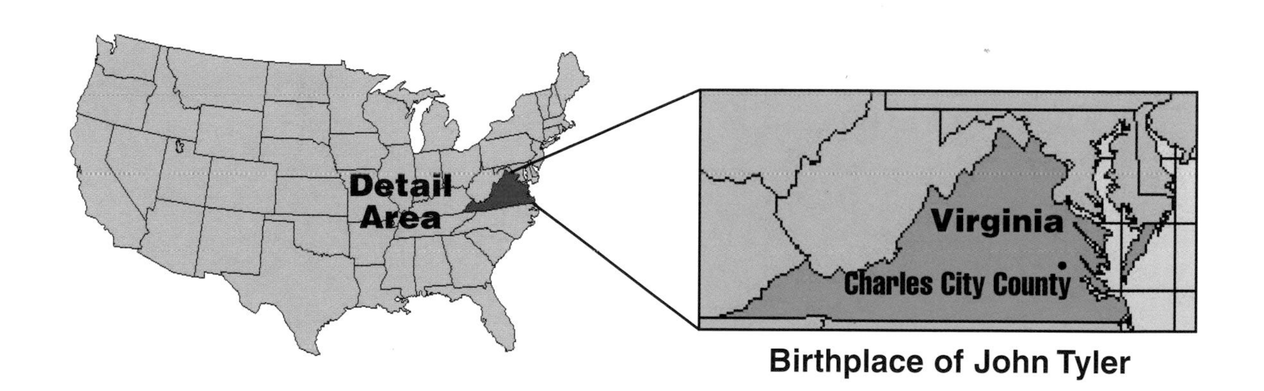


Birthplace of John Tyler

# Early Life

John Tyler was born on March 29, 1790, in Charles City County, Virginia. He was born on a big **plantation** called Greenway.

John's father was also named John. He was a judge. He was once governor of Virginia. John and Mary Tyler had eight children. They were also the **guardians** of 21 other children.

John had blue eyes and light brown hair. He was tall and thin. He liked to write poetry and play the violin. He was gentle and polite, but he could be strong and stubborn. When John was 11, he fought back against a teacher who was beating students.

***John Tyler's birthplace in Charles City County, Virginia***

# The College of William and Mary

In 1802, John began studying at the College of William and Mary. John studied history, law, and politics. He also thought of becoming a violinist.

John graduated from college in 1807 at the age of 17. He studied law with his father. By the time he was 19, John had become a lawyer.

***Opposite page: The College of William and Mary***

# Family Man

*I*n 1808, Tyler fell in love with Letitia Christian. Five years later, on his twenty-third birthday, they were married. They had eight children.

Tyler worked as a lawyer for four years. But soon he became interested in politics. In 1811, Tyler was elected to the Virginia House of **Delegates**.

The next year, the **War of 1812** started. Congressman Tyler supported this war against Great Britain. In 1813, Tyler became a captain in the local **militia**. He was in charge of the Charles City Rifles. They defended the city against the British.

In 1816, Tyler was elected to the U.S. **House of Representatives**. He moved to Washington, D.C.

In **Congress**, Tyler spoke out against the Bank of the United States. The bank had been created in 1816 to give loans to the national government and state banks. Tyler believed the Constitution did not give the national government the power to form this bank. But in 1819, the Supreme Court upheld the creation of the bank.

Tyler also voted against the Missouri Compromise of 1820. The Compromise decided how far slavery could spread in America. Tyler did not believe that the national government or Northern states should interfere with slavery.

**_Letitia Christian Tyler_**

Tyler stayed in Congress for four years. He quit in 1821 because of poor health. In 1823, after getting his strength back, he was elected to the Virginia House of **Delegates**. He served there until 1825.

# *The Making of the Tenth United States President*

Born March 29 in Charles City County, Virginia

Begins studying at College of William and Mary

Graduates from college

Marries Letitia Christian

**1816**

Elected to the U.S. House of Representatives

**1823**

Elected to the Virginia House of Delegates

**1825**

Elected governor of Virginia

**1841**

Harrison dies; Tyler becomes President

**1842**

Wife Letitia dies

**1844**

Marries Julia Gardiner; Polk elected president

**PRESIDENTIAL YEARS**

# John Tyler

*"The institutions under which we live, my countrymen, secure each person in the perfect enjoyment of all his rights."*

Begins law practice

**1811**

Elected to the Virginia House of Delegates

**1827**

Elected to U.S. Senate

**1840**

Elected vice president under William Henry Harrison

**1845**

Retires to Sherwood Forest

**1861**

Civil War begins; elected to Confederate House of Representatives

**1862**

Dies January 18

## Historic Events during Tyler's Presidency

YMCA founded in England by George Williams

First long-distance telegraph line opened between Washington and Baltimore

*A Christmas Carol* by Charles Dickens is published

# From Democrat to Whig

*I*n 1825, the state **legislature** chose John Tyler to be the governor of Virginia. As governor, he supported the improvement of roads and schools. He wanted to unite Virginia's counties with roads and canals.

But Virginia's constitution gave more power to the state **congress** than to the governor. The congress did not support Tyler's plans. In 1827, Tyler was elected to the U.S. Senate and he moved back to Washington, D.C.

Tyler was a **Democrat**. He supported Democrat Andrew Jackson for president in 1828. But President Jackson removed government money from the Bank of the United States and deposited it in state banks.

Tyler claimed the president did not have constitutional power to do this. Tyler voted to **censure** Jackson.

The Virginia **legislature** told Tyler to change his vote. Tyler refused, and quit the Senate in 1836. He returned to Virginia to be a lawyer.

***Andrew Jackson***

# "Tippecanoe and Tyler, Too!"

In 1834, a new political party was formed. It was called the **Whig** party. It was mostly made up of **Democrats** who were upset with the government's interpretation of the Constitution.

In 1839, Whig party candidate William Henry Harrison ran for president. People liked Harrison because he had won the Battle of Tippecanoe during the **War of 1812**.

William Harrison was from the North. The Whig party also needed Southern votes to win the election. So, the Whigs asked Tyler, a Virginian, to run as vice president.

The 1840 campaign changed the way political campaigns were run. During the campaign, the candidates avoided political issues. Instead, the **Whigs** used songs, trinkets, and gimmicks to get votes.

The jingle for the Whig campaign was "Tippecanoe and Tyler, Too!" Harrison's nickname was "Old Tippecanoe," after the battle. The jingle made his nickname and his running mate's name fun to say and easy to remember.

Though the people did not know what Harrison and Tyler stood for, they remembered the songs and free trinkets. Harrison and Tyler won the election. But only one month after taking office, President Harrison died.

*William Henry Harrison*

# President Tyler

Nobody knew what to do next. No president had ever died in office before.

The Constitution said if a president left office, the vice president became the president. But for how long?

Some people thought there should be another election. They thought Tyler could not remain president because he was not elected into that office. But Tyler claimed it was his constitutional right to remain president until the next election.

On April 6, 1841, Tyler took the oath of office and became president. **Congress** finally passed **resolutions** recognizing Tyler's right to remain in office. Tyler's successful fight set the course for future vice presidents who would assume the power of the presidency.

Tyler and **Congress** did not agree on much while he was president. Many lawmakers still felt that he wasn't really the president. Tyler did not agree with many of the laws Congress wrote. So, he **vetoed** them. His nickname became "Old Veto."

**Whig** leaders were not pleased with Tyler. He fought their plans as well. So, they **expelled** him from the party in 1841.

In 1842, Letitia Tyler died. In 1844, Tyler married Julia Gardiner. He was the first president to get married while in office. John and Julia had five sons and two daughters.

***A portrait of President John Tyler***

Despite his battles with **Congress**, President Tyler accomplished many things. He negotiated the Treaty of Wanghia with China in 1844. This treaty opened trade between the two nations. In 1845, Florida became a state. And Congress passed a joint resolution for the **annexation** of Texas.

When Tyler was president, Congress passed the Postal Reform Act on March 3, 1845. This act let the government buy private post offices and make them U.S. post offices. This improved delivery service. The act also lowered the cost of sending mail. And it provided two navy steam ships to deliver mail to other countries.

President Tyler supported improvement of the U.S. Navy. He helped the navy get money for new ships and equipment. The USS *Princeton* was the United States' first steam-powered warship made of iron.

Despite his accomplishments, Tyler was not nominated by the **Whigs** or the **Democrats** in 1844. He left office in 1845.

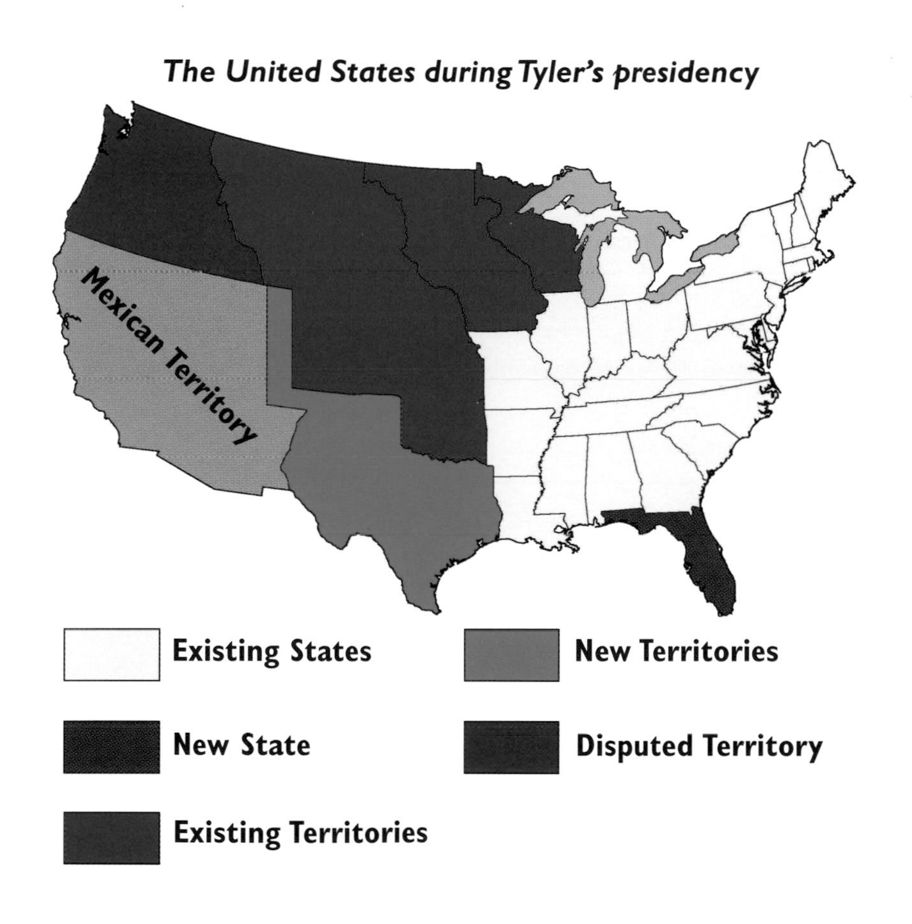

# The Seven "Hats" of the U.S. President

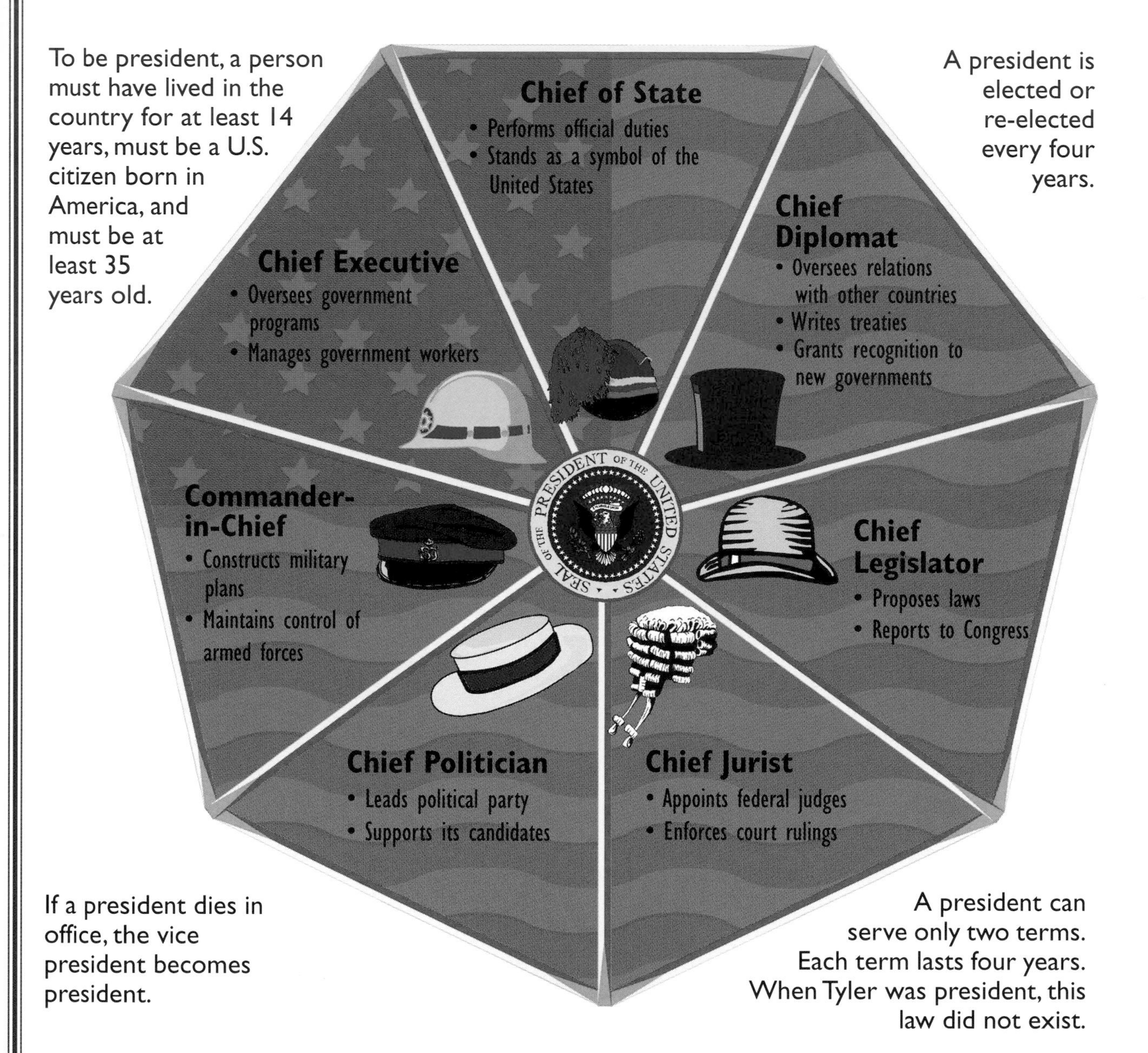


***As president, John Tyler had seven jobs.***

# The Three Branches of the U.S. Government

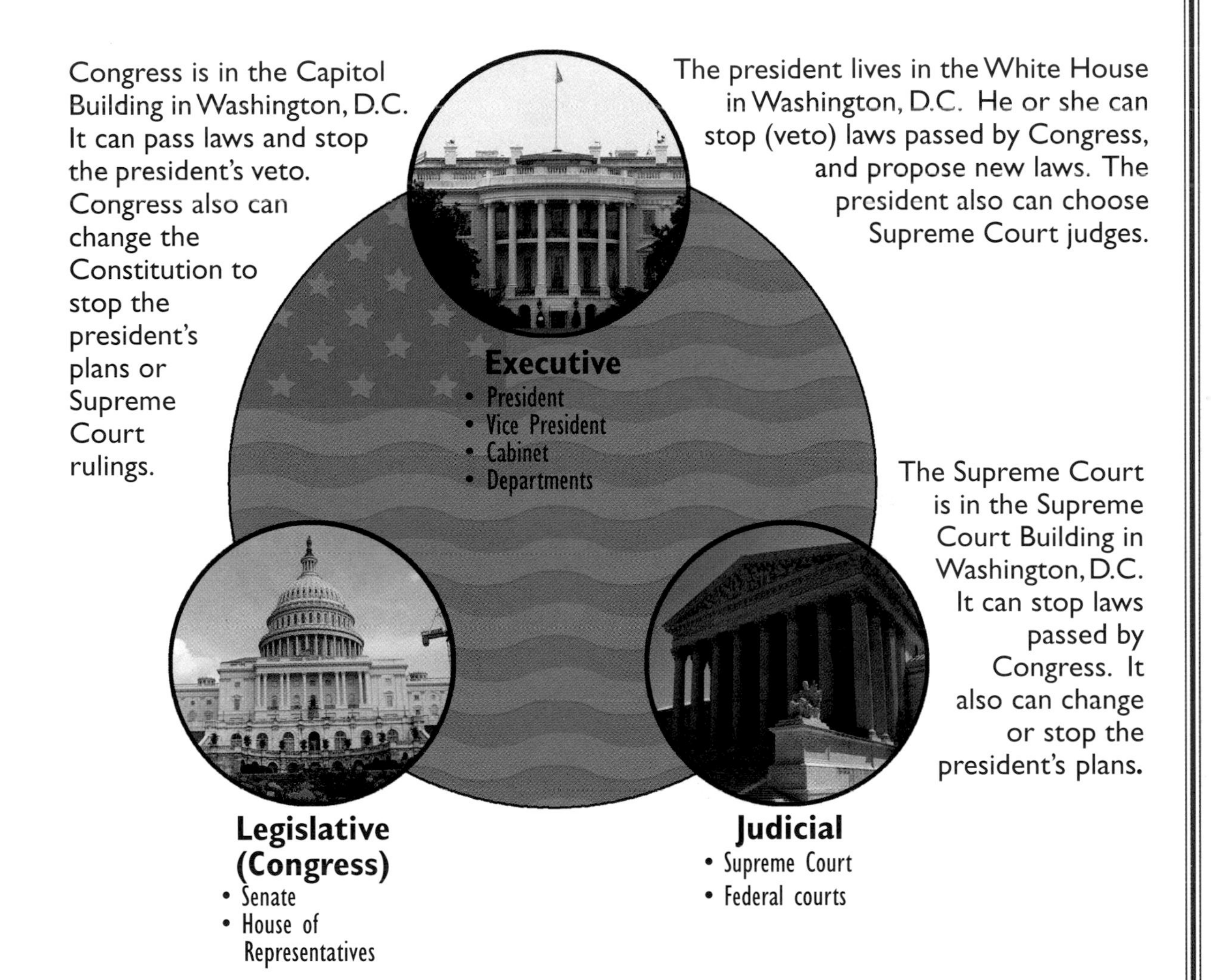


***The U.S. Constitution formed three government branches. Each branch has power over the others. So, no single group or person can control the country. The Constitution calls this "separation of powers."***

# After the White House

When Tyler left the White House, his family moved to Sherwood Forest, a big home not far from Greenway. Tyler lived there quietly for many years.

But Americans argued more and more about slavery. In 1861, Tyler led a conference that tried to find a solution. He believed that each state had the right to decide whether or not to allow slavery.

Tyler feared that the South would leave the Union and form its own country. He argued against such a decision. But he did not succeed.

In 1861, Abraham Lincoln became president. The Southern states **seceded** from the Union. They called their new country the **Confederate States of America**. The **Civil War** had begun.

John Tyler was elected to the Confederate **House of Representatives** in May 1861. But before he could takc his position, hc dicd on January 18, 1862.

John Tyler was the first vice president to reach the presidency because of a president's death. His successful fight to remain in office set the course for future vice presidents who assumed presidential power. In 1933, **Congress** finally amended the Constitution to allow the vice president to finish the term of a president who dies in office.

***John Tyler's home, Sherwood Forest***

# Fun Facts

- John Tyler was in the **War of 1812** for a short time. Later, he liked to tell a story about one night when he and the other men were asleep. In the middle of the night, there was a false alarm that the enemy was coming. Tyler jumped up so fast that he fell down the stairs in the dark. This was the worst injury he got in the war!
- John Tyler met his second wife, Julia Gardiner, at a party being held on a ship.
- John Tyler, born in March 1790, was the first president to be born after the end of the **Revolutionary War**.

- Julia Gardiner Tyler liked to have big parties at the White House. Sometimes, when John arrived at the party, she had the band play a song called "Hail to the Chief." Today, that song is still played for the President of the United States.

*A rare photo of John Tyler*

# Glossary

**annex** - to add land to a nation.

**cabinet** - a group of advisers chosen by the president.

**censure** - an official expression of disapproval.

**Civil War** - 1861 to 1865. A war between the Union and the Confederate States of America.

**Confederate States of America** - the country formed by the 11 southern states that left the Union between 1860 and 1861.

**Congress** - the lawmaking body of the United States. It is made up of the Senate and the House of Representatives. Most states also have a congress.

**delegate** - a person who represents voters.

**Democrat** - a political party. During the 1800s it was conservative and supported farmers and landowners.

**expel** - to throw out.

**guardian** - a person who helps take care of children who have lost their own parents.

**House of Representatives** - a group of people elected by citizens to represent them. They meet in Washington, D.C., and make laws for the country.

**legislature** - the lawmaking group of a country or state.

**militia** - citizens trained for war or emergencies. The National Guard.

**plantation** - a large farm that grows crops such as tobacco, cotton, or sugarcane.

**resolution** - an official expression of opinion or will.

**Revolutionary War** - 1775 to 1783. A war fought between Great Britain and its thirteen American colonies over the colonies' independence.

**secede** - to break away from a group.

**veto** - to keep a law or vote from passing. Veto is a special power held by the president. Congress can overrule a veto with a two-thirds majority vote.

**War of 1812** - 1812-1814. A war fought between the U.S. and Great Britain over shipping and the capture of U.S. sailors.

**Whig** - a political party that was very strong in the early 1800s, but ended in the 1850s. They supported laws that helped business.

# Internet Sites

**United States Presidents Information Page**
**http://historyoftheworld.com/soquel/prez.htm**
Links to information about United States presidents. This site is very informative, with biographies on every president as well as speeches and debates, and other links.

**The Presidents of the United States of America**
**http://www.whitehouse.gov/WH/glimpse/presidents/html/presidents.html**
This site is from the White House. With an introduction from President Bill Clinton and biographies that include each president's inaugural address, this site is excellent. Get information on White House history, art in the White House, first ladies, first families, and much more.

**POTUS—Presidents of the United States**
**http://www.ipl.org/ref/POTUS/**
In this resource you will find background information, election results, cabinet members, presidency highlights, and some odd facts on each of the presidents. Links to biographies, historical documents, audio and video files, and other presidential sites are also included to enrich this site.

*These sites are subject to change. Go to your favorite search engine and type in United States presidents for more sites.*

# Pass It On

History enthusiasts: educate readers around the country by passing on information you've learned about presidents or other important people who've changed history. Share your little-known facts and interesting stories. We want to hear from you!

To get posted on the ABDO Publishing Company Web site, email us at:
**history@abdopub.com**
Visit the ABDO Publishing Company Web site at www.abdopub.com

# Index